Our Lady of Prompt Succor and the Battle of New Orleans

Copyright © 2024 by JSB Morse. All Rights Reserved. Printed in the United States of America.

This book was produced by Libertas Kids, an Imprint of Code Publishing, Austin, TX. LibertasKids.com
ISBN 978-1-60020-115-8 Ebook ISBN 978-1-60020-116-5

1788
New Orleans, Louisiana

The Ursuline Sisters had been helping the City of New Orleans for over 60 years in their school and orphanage when, on Good Friday, 1788, they faced their gravest challenge.

A terrible fire was roaring through the city and headed straight for the Ursuline Convent. The sisters were ordered to evacuate, but the nuns did not want to leave their home to be destroyed.

One nun, Sister St. Anthony, found a small statue of Our Lady and, staring down the fire, the sisters prayed, "Our Lady of Prompt Succor, we are lost unless you hasten to our aid!" Within minutes, the direction of the wind changed and slowed the rapid spread of the flames, and the fire was soon extinguished. The convent remained unharmed even though the majority of the surrounding structures were consumed by flames. Witnesses were amazed, exclaiming, "Our Lady of Prompt Succor has saved us!"

Years later, the convent was in grave need of assistance. Many of the Ursuline Sisters had fled to Cuba due to fear of religious persecution when Napoleon captured the territory from Spain in 1800. After the loss of their beloved Mother Superior, only a small handful of nuns were left to care for the immense responsibility of the convent, school, and orphanage. The newly-appointed Mother St. André was overwhelmed and called upon the help of Our Lady.

Gazing upon a small painting of the serene countenance of the Madonna and Child, Mother St. André prayed. "Most clement and sweet Mother, we are in desperate need of quick help. If it is the will of your Son, please send us aid!" She then wrote to her cousin in France to bring help to the New World.

1808
Montpelier, France

Mother St. Michel Gensoul was a pious woman of great sanctity who gracefully endured many hardships during the French Revolution. After her forceful removal from the Pont-Saint-Espirit monastery, she was able to found a flourishing school for girls in Montpelier in the South of France. On a sunny afternoon, Mother St. Michel received the letter from her cousin Mother St. André in New Orleans.

She had a sincere desire to help the distressed sisters in New Orleans, so Mother St. Michel asked her bishop if she could sail across the ocean with more nuns to help her cousin. Fearing the fate of the girls' school, the bishop said that only the pope could make that decision.

Communicating with the pontiff would prove a difficult task, however, because Napoleon had occupied the Eternal City with his troops with plans to imprison the pope.

Despite the seemingly impossible circumstances, Mother St. Michel petitioned the pope and turned to Our Lady for help. She promised to have a statue made honoring Mary under the title of Our Lady of Prompt Succor if her prayer was answered quickly.

Amazingly, Pope Pius VII received the request just days before being imprisoned by Napoleon and cut off from the outside world, he speedily approved Mother St. Michel's request.

Faithful to her word, Mother St. Michel had a statue of Our Lady constructed and brought it with her and several sisters to New Orleans in 1810. Reunited with her cousin, Mother St. Michel became immersed in the arduous work at the convent. These humble and steadfast women were unknowingly about to change the course of history in New Orleans and beyond.

1815
New Orleans, Louisiana

A few years later, the British had just burned Washington, DC to the ground in its war with the United States, and had its sights set on the thriving port of New Orleans next. It was the worst threat New Orleans had ever faced: 8,000 of the world's most powerful military.

Defending New Orleans would be a rag-tag collection of 5,700 soldiers that consisted of Tennessee and Kentucky frontiersmen, Louisiana militia, New Orleans businessmen, free men of color, Choctaw Indians, smuggler Jean Lafitte and his privateers, sailors, marines, and United States troops led by the young General Andrew Jackson.

Seeing how dire the situation was and how dim the prospect of victory was, the Ursulines turned once again to Our Lady of Prompt Succor, rallying the entire community to join them in fervent prayer.

The new superior, Mother St. Marie Olivier de Vezin, promised Our Lady that if Jackson and his men were victorious, a Mass of thanksgiving would be sung every year in memory of her saving help to the city on that day.

On January 7, 1815, the night before the Battle of New Orleans, the statue of Our Lady of Prompt Succor was placed above the chapel entrance. All night long the Ursuline sisters and New Orleans citizens prayed in the Chapel of Our Lady of Consolation while awaiting word from the Chalmette battlefield a few miles away.

The British attacked before dawn on January 8, hoping to surprise the Americans under cover of a thick fog. But the fog miraculously lifted, giving American rifle and artillerymen clear sight lines.

Each advance by the British was met with fierce resistance by the Americans and within only thirty minutes, the Americans had won the battle. The assault cost the British some 2,000 casualties, including three generals and seven colonels. Amazingly, Jackson's outfit of frontiersmen and regulars had lost just 13 men in the stunning surprise victory.

As dawn painted the sky a celestial blue, Bishop DuBourg began Mass. At the very moment of Communion, a courier burst into the chapel, heralding the victory of Jackson and his men. The chapel resounded with a jubilant rendition of the Te Deum.

News of a peace treaty soon followed and General Jackson wrote a letter to Bishop DuBourg calling for a gathering of all citizens to give thanks for "the great assistance we have received from the Ruler of all events."

Pope Pius IX authorized the public devotion to the Marian title of Our Lady of Prompt Succor on 21 September 1851 and designated the 8th of January as its feast day of thanksgiving. Pope Leo XIII later granted a Canonical Coronation to the image through Archbishop Francis Janssens on 10 November 1895.

For more great books visit LibertasKids.com

www.ingramcontent.com/pod-product-compliance
Lightning Source LLC
Chambersburg PA
CBHW041603070526
44586CB00003BA/62